Across Five Aprils

Study Guide

by Carol Clark

For the novel by Irene Hunt

For easier classroom or co-op use or distance learning with Progeny Press study guides, check out our interactive eGuide downloads, available at www.progenypress.com.

Across Five Aprils Study Guide
A Progeny Press Study Guide
by Carol Clark
edited by Rebecca Gilleland and Michael Gilleland
cover design by Mary Duban and Michael Gilleland

Product of the United States of America.

ISBN: 978-1-58609-204-7 Book
978-1-58609-590-1 CD
978-1-58609-736-3 eGuide

Table of Contents

Study Guide Author 5
Note to Instructor 6
Synopsis 8
About the Novel's Author 9
Background Information 10
Ideas for Prereading Activities 12
Activities During Reading 13
Chapters 1 & 2 14
Chapters 3 & 4 23
Chapters 5 & 6 31
Chapters 7 & 8 39
Chapters 9 & 10 44
Chapters 11 & 12 50
Overview 57
Essay and Writing Suggestions 60
Additional Resources 63
Answer Key 65

Study Guide Author

Mrs. Carol Clark teaches junior high school language arts at Toledo Christian School in northwest Ohio. Her passions are helping kids learn, teaching great literature, and encouraging kids to grow in their relationship with Jesus Christ.

Mrs. Clark earned her B.A. in English education at Bloomfield College and her M.Ed. in elementary and early childhood education at the University of Toledo. She enjoys playing classical music on the piano, reading, writing, and playing with her three grandsons. Mrs. Clark is involved in outreach ministries through her local church, including baking cookies for and writing letters to servicemen in Iraq; making casseroles for the Good Samaritan Center, which services the poor of Toledo; and directing a kids' outreach program in Appalachia on a missions trip with World Servants. In addition to classroom teaching, Mrs. Clark has worked as secretary and editor for some of the most creative engineers in the United States and has edited for two magazines and a technical journal. She has also published interviews and articles in several magazines.

Note to Instructor

How to Use Progeny Press Study Guides. Progeny Press study guides are designed to help students better understand and enjoy literature by getting them to notice and understand how authors craft their stories and to show them how to think through the themes and ideas introduced in the stories. To properly work through a Progeny Press study guide, students should have easy access to a good dictionary, a thesaurus, a Bible (we use NIV translation, but that is up to your preference; just be aware of some differences in language), and sometimes a topical Bible or concordance. Supervised access to the Internet also can be helpful at times, as can a good set of encyclopedias.

Most middle grades and high school study guides take from eight to ten weeks to complete, generally working on one section per week. Over the years, we have found that it works best if the students completely read the novel the first week, while also working on a prereading activity chosen by the parent or teacher. Starting the second week, most parents and teachers have found it works best to work on one study guide page per day until the chapter sections are completed. Students should be allowed to complete questions by referring to the book; many questions require some cross-reference between elements of the stories.

Most study guides contain an Overview section that can be used as a final test, or it can be completed in the same way the chapter sections were completed. If you wish to perform a final test but your particular study guide does not have an Overview section, we suggest picking a couple of questions from each section of the study guide and using them as your final test.

Most study guides also have a final section of essays and postreading activities. These may be assigned at the parents' or teachers' discretion, but we suggest that students engage in several writing or other extra activities during the study of the novel to complement their reading and strengthen their writing skills.

As for high school credits, most Christian high schools to whom we have spoken have assigned a value of one-fourth credit to each study guide, and this also seems to be acceptable to colleges assessing homeschool transcripts.

Internet References

All websites listed in this study guide were checked for appropriateness at the time of publication. However, due to the changing nature of the Internet, we cannot guarantee that the URLs listed will remain appropriate or viable. Therefore, we urge parents and teachers to take care in and exercise careful oversight of their children's use of the Internet.

Synopsis

Times are uneasy for the Matthew Creighton family as tensions rise between the north and the south as the war between the states approaches. The Creightons and their neighbors in southern Illinois have friends and relatives on both sides of the issues. The younger sons look forward to the gallantry and excitement they believe war will bring, but Matthew and his older sons better understand war's cost. When war breaks out, the Creighton boys head off to fight, expecting a quick and easy victory for the north. But when an older son, Bill, goes off to fight for the south, the Creightons find the war has divided their family and brought dangerous strife between neighbors.

Nine-year-old Jethro Creighton suddenly finds himself the only remaining son in the family, and when his father suffers a heart attack, Jethro becomes the working man of the family. Times are hard and the work endless, but their thoughts always are with their boys in the war. They seem to live from letter to letter and for each newspaper with accounts of the fighting.

With boys on both sides of the war, the Creightons also find themselves the target of whichever troublemakers wish to pick a fight. But they also learn that some neighbors remember old kindnesses, and people still will band together against injustice. Young Jethro discovers that a man's good character can be stronger than a gun and last longer than a war.

About the Novel's Author

Irene Hunt was born in Pontiac, Illinois, in 1907. When her father died seven years later, she and her mother moved to her grandparents' farm. There she heard many stories from her grandfather, whose own childhood was deeply affected by the events of the Civil War.

Ms. Hunt earned degrees from the University of Illinois and the University of Minnesota and taught psychology at the University of South Dakota. She returned to Illinois to teach English and French. It was while teaching that she recognized that there was little good historical fiction for youth and decided to write some.

Across Five Aprils, Hunt's first novel and a Newbery Honor book, is based on family letters and records, as well as her grandfather's reminiscences of the Civil War. The novel was published when Hunt was 57 years old. In 1966, two years later, she earned the Newbery Medal for her second novel, *Up a Road Slowly. A Trail of Apple Blossoms* was published in 1968, and *No Promises in the Wind* in 1970. Ms. Hunt died in 2001 at the age of 94.

Background Information

During the years of 1861 through 1865, the United States was engaged in one of the bloodiest wars of her history, the Civil War. Before it ended, 620,000 soldiers would lie dead and another 500,000 would be wounded.

Set in southern Illinois, *Across Five Aprils* confronts the issues and questions that split apart families and friends during those years: Should our state be a slave state or a free state? Should we join this war, and for which side should we fight? Is there a right or wrong side of this war? Will our sons return home safely? Irene Hunt has based this historical fiction novel on stories that her grandfather told her about the Civil War. Yet, she has given an accurate and well-researched account of a number of battles as seen through the eyes of her characters.

While the question of slavery is often offered as the major reason for this war, there were a number of other issues involved. The United States seemed to be at odds with itself even before the war. Northern states were highly industrialized, with factories producing manufactured goods; they had large, well-populated cities; and the railroads were developing into an effective transportation system for both people and products. The Southern economy, on the other hand, was largely dependent on huge plantations that grew cash crops such as cotton and tobacco. In the eyes of Southern landowners, slaves were necessary to do the work of the plantation.

In December 1860, South Carolina seceded (broke away) from the United States, and within the next several months 10 other states followed. They formed their own government, the Confederate States of America, and elected Jefferson Davis as President. The Confederacy established its capital at Richmond, Virginia.

The Civil War began when the South fired on Fort Sumter, in South Carolina, on April 12, 1861. The war was fought on several fronts at the same time. As you read this novel, you will become acquainted with the Army of the Potomac and the Army of the Cumberland. You will also meet a great many generals. U.S. President Abraham Lincoln asked General Robert E. Lee to command the Union forces, but Lee turned him down in favor of his home state of Virginia and led the Southern forces instead. Lincoln then appointed a number of generals in succession, having a difficult time finding one who could successfully command the Northern forces. The strategy of the Union (the North) was to control the Mississippi River and to blockade Southern ports to prevent the movement of troops and supplies, and then to conquer Richmond. The North assumed that the war would end rather quickly, maybe even in several weeks, but it dragged on for four long years until Lee surrendered to General U.S. Grant at Appomattox Court House in Virginia on April 9, 1865.

Ideas for Prereading Activities

You may find additional extension activities, projects, and information on this and other Progeny Press titles at `https://www.pinterest.com/progenypress/boards/`.

1. Research the causes of the U.S. Civil War. Write a short essay comparing and contrasting the economies of the northern and southern states and giving several reasons why each side might choose to go to war.

2. Look for information on the following laws and court cases. How did each one attempt to resolve slavery issues?
   - The Missouri Compromise
   - Kansas-Nebraska Act
   - Dred Scott case

3. *Map work:* Using an encyclopedia, online website, or American history textbook, determine the 11 states which seceded to form the Confederate States. Mark these on a large map of the eastern United States. Which states remained in the Union? Which were considered "border states"? Outline the northern, southern, and border states on your map with marker, using three different colors.

Activities During Reading

1. Become familiar with the beginning of the Civil War and the firing on Fort Sumter by researching via website, encyclopedia, or history textbook.

2. Draw and cut out or purchase a number of miniature Union and Confederate flags. As you read *Across Five Aprils*, place these flags on your map at the sites of the major battles to symbolize the victors of each and to help you track the progress of the war. Small stickers or labels work well.

Chapters 1 & 2

Vocabulary:

Section 1

Look up the following words in a dictionary and write a short definition for each:

1. Calvinism:
2. abolitionist:
3. tariff:
4. secede:

Section 2

A word is in *context* if we read it in the sentence in which it was written. It is *out of context* when it is by itself. The following underlined words are shown in the context of the sentences in which they appear in the book. Read the sentences and try to define the underlined words from the surrounding context. Then look up the dictionary definition and compare your answer.

5. [W]hy should the President waver so long? Why should he refuse, week after week, to start the great explosion which the young men wanted. . . . He sighed suddenly and deeply at his <u>perplexities</u>.
   My definition:

Dictionary definition:

6. He filled a burlap pouch with the potato cuttings and hoisted it expertly to his thin shoulder.
My definition:

Dictionary definition:

7. "Mister, I'd like to get a word in right here." Wilse Graham's voice was strident with anger.
My definition:

Dictionary definition:

8. He had been stricken with typhoid fever during his first year of teaching, and Ellen Creighton had patiently nursed him back to health.
My definition:

Dictionary definition:

9. Jethro, although he was concerned mostly with the goodness of the food he ate, was vaguely aware of a troubled preoccupation all about him.
My definition:

Dictionary definition:

Questions:

1. The *setting* of a novel is the time and place in which it occurs. The time may be general (winter) or specific (November of 1863). The place, or location, may be described briefly or thoroughly, either by the author or the characters themselves. What is the setting of *Across Five Aprils*, as the novel begins?
   Time:

   Place:

2. Who was Copernicus? Why does Jethro introduce the subject of his teachings to his mother? What is her reaction to the teachings? How does she feel about Jethro's explanation?

3. What is Jethro's attitude toward war?

4. Describe the circumstances of Mary Creighton's death.

5. What makes Jethro like Bill so well? What aspects of Bill's character does he admire?

6. Explain Jethro's relationship with his brother John and his wife Nancy.

7. What event begins the Civil War? Which side fires first? Why?

Thinking About the Story:

8. How has the earlier death of three children within one week's time affected the relationship between Ellen Creighton and Jethro, her youngest child? Does she treat him differently, as a result of this experience? If so, why?

9. Explain the honor of "first table" that is extended to Jethro at the end of potato planting. What is significant about Bill's handing him bread dipped in coffee?

10. When Wilse Graham visits, the Creightons discuss the impending war before the first shots are fired. Reread their conversations around the supper table, and list the differing opinions of each family member concerning the war and slavery issues.

    Wilse:

    John:

Bill:

Matt:

Ellen:

11. Writers often create special effects by using a literary technique called *similes.* A simile is a comparison of two unlike things in which a word of comparison (*like* or *as*) is used. For example: The runner sped down the track *like* a bolt of lightning. The runner is being compared to a bolt of lightning. In each passage below, underline the simile, then tell what is compared.

    a. "Three of her children died within one week of the dreaded disease they called child's paralysis, a disease which struck the country that year, people said, like the soldiers of Herod."

    ______________________ is compared to ______________________

    b. "War meant loud brass music and shining horses ridden by men wearing uniforms finer than any suit in the stores at Newton; it meant men riding like kings, looking neither to the right nor the left, while lesser men in perfect lines strode along with guns across their shoulders, their heads held high like horses with short reins."

    ______________________ are compared to ______________________

    ______________________ are compared to ______________________

c. "Jenny's voice came clearly, pleasant as the sound of a little bell ringing."

________________________ is compared to ________________________

d. "Huge silver poplars towered above the cabin, their roots extending like giant claws."

________________________ are compared to ________________________

e. It was a coveted honor and he accepted it with dignity, looking somewhat like a solemn dwarf as he sat between his father and Bill, his eyes wide beneath the tumble of yellow curls that clung to his forehead and the back of his neck.

________________________ is compared to ________________________

f. "'He [Bill] talked to it [his horse] gentle,' the story went, 'like a woman talkin' to a young 'un.'"

________________________ is compared to ________________________

Idioms:

An *idiom* is an expression that does not literally mean what it says but has a different, understood, meaning. For example, if you say you are *hanging around* the park, we know that you aren't literally *hanging*. Idioms, like *dialects,* are often peculiar to a region. Hunts' use of idioms in *Across Five Aprils* helps bring to life the setting of the story. Underlined in the sentences below are some of the idioms found in the story. Explain what each of the idioms means according to the context of the sentence.

12. Shad says that some folks took that news real hard; it kind of let the <u>wind out of their sails</u> all of a sudden.

13. Well, <u>the pot can't call the kettle black</u>—look what we're stirrin' up amongst ourselves.

14. "<u>He'd put his hand in the fire fer you</u>, Jeth," she told him once, and Jethro believed her.

15. Yore own Ol' Abe from this fair state of Illinois <u>is talkin' out of both sides of his mouth</u>—fer the time bein' anyway.

16. Now he kin set back and look pious at the states that <u>has been blowin' hot and cold.</u>

Dig Deeper:

17. Describe the Burdow family. Why are they disliked by the citizens of Jasper County?

18. Jethro is perplexed when his father halts an act of revenge against the Burdows. Why is Jethro upset? In what way does his father's intervention with the angry crowd remind him of the President's actions with regard to the Civil War?

19. Read Psalm 103:8–10 and Romans 12:19–21. How do these verses illustrate Matthew Creighton's response to Mary's death?

20. Read Ezekiel 18:19–20. What do these verses tell us? Considering this, was Travis Burdow treated fairly by the community? Why or why not?

21. *Characterization:* Irene Hunt, the author of *Across Five Aprils*, introduces us to the important characters of this novel largely through their own conversations. We also learn about their thoughts and feelings as Jethro wrestles through different issues, or by the author's direct commentary on events of the times. What does the following quotation reveal about Ellen Creighton's character?

> . . . there were reverberations of Calvinism strong within her, which would have protested vigorously against the vanity of regret for a passing beauty. She had borne twelve children, four of whom were dead . . . she had lived through sickness, poverty, and danger for over thirty years; the sight of a pretty face might bring a tired smile to her lips, but it was a thing of little value in Ellen's world.

22. After Mary was killed on the way home from the dance, the crowd was intent on revenge. What does Matthew Creighton's intervention teach us about his character?

Optional Writing Activities:

1. Write one to two paragraphs about a time when you were tempted to react negatively toward a classmate or an acquaintance. How did the actions or attitudes of your friends influence your behavior? Looking back on this situation, evaluate whether your responses were appropriate in light of the above Bible verses.

2. Describe what might have happened if the crowd had not listened to Matthew Creighton and had decided to seek revenge on the Burdow family for Mary's death. What are the possible results from such actions?

Chapters 3 & 4

Connections to History:

Choose one or more of the following projects to do as you read.

1. Look up some of the important military leaders of the Civil War in an encyclopedia or on-line source. Present the significant accomplishments of several of the following. This could be presented individually or in teams as an oral or written report or as an informational poster:

   - Jefferson Davis
   - Robert E. Lee
   - Ulysses S. Grant
   - George Meade
   - William Tecumseh Sherman
   - Abraham Lincoln

2. On your map of the eastern United States, trace Shadrach's explanation of the strategy of the Union. You might find it helpful to mark this with a colored pencil.

3. As the novel progresses, the characters will learn the results of a number of battles of the ongoing Civil War. Investigate these early battles and briefly explain them and their importance to the outcome of the war:

   - The Battle of Bull Run
   - The Battles at Fort Henry and Fort Donelson

4. Add flags or markings to your map to indicate the victors of each of the above battles.

Vocabulary:

Word List

blithely	bunting	denounce	emancipator	fiasco
nullify	oratory	prestige	quavering	resolve
	sullen		wastrel	

The *synonym* of a word is a different word with a similar meaning. *Synonyms* are given below for each of the above vocabulary words. Write the correct vocabulary word from the Word List on each line. Use a dictionary to learn the meaning of each word you do not know.

1. ______________________________ prominence, fame, pre-eminence
2. ______________________________ determination, intention, purpose
3. ______________________________ failure, wreck
4. ______________________________ cheerfully, happily, carefree
5. ______________________________ streamer, banner
6. ______________________________ trembling, quivering
7. ______________________________ invalidate, annul
8. ______________________________ sulky, glum

9. __________________________ liberator, rescuer

10. __________________________ talk, speech, rhetoric

11. __________________________ accuse, condemn, charge

12. __________________________ waster, spendthrift

Questions:

1. Look up the Mason-Dixon line. What was it? Why was it important to the Civil War?

2. Which two family members first leave home to join the fighting? For which side do they enlist?

3. Why is General Frémont both praised and criticized?

4. Why is Jethro sometimes afraid at night? How is he comforted?

5. Why does Matthew Creighton not approve of Jethro's playing on Walnut Hill?

6. On what two occasions are bells rung throughout northern cities during February of 1862? Who is the victorious general they honored?

7. Describe the circumstances that earn General Grant the nickname of "Unconditional Surrender Grant."

Thinking About the Story:

8. How does the news of early Union defeats at Bull Run and Ball's Bluff change people's ideas about the outcome and the length of the Civil War?

9. As Bill talks with Jethro to calm his fears in the middle of the night, why does Jethro suddenly feel "desolate and alone"? What does this conversation reveal about Bill's dilemma over going to war, his attitude toward slavery, and his thoughts about secession? Why do you think Bill chooses the South?

10. Tom's letter home records a decision made by some of the soldiers on the way to Fort Donelson. Explain the decision and the circumstances behind it. How does this choice affect Tom's response to the Union victory at the fort?

11. Sometimes authors create special effects in their writing by using literary techniques. One technique is *personification,* in which the author speaks of or describes an animal, object, or idea as if it were a person. For example, "The tree pointed its icy fingers skyward," describes a tree as if it had human hands. Look for and write down an example of personification in the author's description of autumn on Walnut Hill.

12. Look for and write down an example of personification in the paragraph in which Bill's face is cut and a shout is heard.

13. Another technique authors sometimes use is *foreshadowing.* Foreshadowing gives the reader a hint of something to come in the future. Predict what you think may happen in the future, based on each of the following examples of foreshadowing.

    a. ". . . all these once familiar sounds had taken on overtones of wailing, and he seemed to hear an echo of that wailing now. He shivered and looked away from his brother's face."

    b. "Listen to me, Jeth; you're gittin' to be a sizeable boy. There's goin' to be a lot of things in the years ahead that you'll have to stand. There'll be things that tear you apart, but you'll have to stand 'em. You can't count on cryin' to make 'em right."

14. Reread Shadrach Yale's explanation to Jethro of the movement of the Union armies. What basic strategy did the North employ in Kentucky? Explain why control of the Mississippi River was so important to northern success in the Civil War.

15. How has Walnut Hill changed from a place of childhood pleasure to a place of sadness for Jethro?

16. Why does Shadrach rebuke Jethro for calling the president "Ol' Abe"? What are some of the things about which people are criticizing the president? Why do you think Jethro calls the president "Ol' Abe"?

Dig Deeper:

17. In Chapter 3, Tom and Eb go off to war with pride and certainty in their rightness. Bill decides he must go against his father and brothers and fight for the South if he must fight, but he tells Jethro, "I mistrust myself, I mistrust my way of thinkin' when I see how sure they be." In Proverbs 14:12, the Bible says, "There is a way that seems right to a man, but in the end it leads to death." What does this verse mean, and how might it apply to the brothers' discussions and decisions?

What does this verse mean to you, in your own life?

18. As Jethro walks through the bitter cold to share Tom's letter with Shadrach Yale, the author writes, ". . . suffering at the mercy of the elements was accepted by Jethro as being quite as natural as the hunger for green vegetables and fresh fruit that was always with him during the winter. . . . The hardships one endured had a purpose; his mother had been careful to make him aware of that." What purpose might Jethro see in enduring the cold?

19. Read James 1:2–5. When we endure hardships, God may use them to serve a purpose. According to these verses, what are some of the character qualities that, through hardships, God is able to develop in us?

Optional Writing Activities:

1. Looking back over your life, what situations have been difficult for you to endure? How might God have used these to build character in your life? Seeing what you gained from past hardships, how might this knowledge help you in future difficult times?

2. Reread the "Seven Stars" song that Shadrach sings to Jethro. When Jethro expresses his mother's thoughts about the song, Shad offers a differing viewpoint. Explain these two views, and then express your own opinion about why the words to the song don't seem to make sense.

3. In Chapter 4 we see the start of a series of letters that come to the Creighton family from their sons in the military, letters that mean a lot to the family. Letters from home also can be very important reminders to our soldiers of the people back home and the reasons they are in their country's service. Individually or as a class, begin writing letters or e-mails to soldiers from your area that are serving oversees. Try to get to know them and write letters that tell them what is going on back home in your area.

Chapters 5 & 6

Vocabulary:

Read these sentences from the book, then answer the question about the underlined word by writing the letter from the correct response in the blank.

1. Ellen was appalled at the expense.
   When people are appalled, they are _____.
   a. amused and entertained
   b. amazed and astounded
   c. revolted, shocked, and horrified
   d. thrilled and excited
   e. saddened and quieted

2. He had fifteen miles to travel; master of his team, navigator of his route, he felt proud and exhilarated by his freedom and sense of adventure.
   When you are exhilarated, you are _____.
   a. enlivened, elated, delighted.
   b. burdened, responsible
   c. frightened, overwhelmed, oppressed
   d. witty, clever, brilliant
   e. wearied, fatigued, worn

3. People were moving about their morning chores in barnyards or woodlots; inevitably they stood still, watching the approach of the wagon as it rattled down the road; . . .
   When something is inevitable, it is _____.

a. restless, shifting
b. certain, unavoidable
c. envied, admired
d. reluctant, hesitant
e. amusing, humorous

4. Sometimes the wagon wheels sank deep in the mud of a low, wet spot along the road; now and then a wheel passed over a stone or a stump hidden by weeds or tangled vines, and the wagon with its load tilted <u>precariously</u>.
   When something is precarious, it is _____.
   a. special, valuable
   b. silent, unheard
   c. unsteady, perilous
   d. horrid, shocking
   e. disciplined, controlled

5. The man looked as if he had lived in filth for a lifetime, and Jethro felt a <u>loathing</u> that was new to him.
   If you feel loathing, you feel _____.
   a. sick, ill
   b. cold, unfeeling
   c. frustration
   d. shaky, unsteady
   e. hatred, disgust

6. "And I'm goin' with you, Guy," one of the men said, getting to his feet. He turned <u>belligerently</u> when he reached the door.
   If you are belligerent, you are _____.
   a. clumsy, heavy
   b. quick, brisk, light on your feet
   c. carefree, happy, buoyant
   d. defiant, angry, hostile
   e. aloof, uncaring

7. "You're a very <u>astute</u> woman, Lily, but like most of us, you have your blind spots."
   If someone is astute, they are _____.
   a. pained, afflicted, suffering
   b. solid, reliable, dependable
   c. discerning, acute, shrewd
   d. contrary, opposing, antagonistic
   e. delicate, tender, gentle

8. Southern Illinois was beginning to feel the <u>tumult</u> that had rocked Missouri.
   If one feels tumult, one feels _____.
   a. fortunate, lucky, favored
   b. turmoil, disturbance, trouble
   c. incomplete, unfinished, deficient
   d. alien, foreign, external
   e. included, admitted, embraced

9. He found himself nodding a little now and then as the slow creak of the wheels invited sleep, and he had to shake himself briskly and to talk aloud for a while when the <u>monotony</u> became overpowering.
   If you are overpowered by monotony, you are overpowered by _____.
   a. repetition, boring similarity
   b. exhaustion, weakness, feebleness
   c. daydreams, fancies, whims
   d. discomfort, soreness, pain
   e. chilliness, cold, rawness

10. There was no sound but the creaking of the wagon as it <u>floundered</u> through the sour-smelling mud and over mammoth tree roots.
    If something begins to flounder, it begins to _____.
    a. weep, cry, wail
    b. glide, float
    c. slow, pause
    d. wallow, sway, stagger
    e. sink, submerge

11. He was afraid, but his fear was vague, and anger was as strong as fear when he thought of the precious bag of coffee and of the little gifts. . . .
    If something is vague, it is _____.
    a. gripping, overwhelming
    b. determined, resolved
    c. thin, scanty, meager
    d. terrifying, dismaying, horrifying
    e. indefinite, ambiguous

12. Both man and boy seemed to be in tacit agreement that the attack at the bridge was a closed incident, a thing for which they felt a solid indifference.
    If you feel indifference for something, you feel _____.
    a. loathing, hatred
    b. lack of interest or concern
    c. fear, apprehension
    d. bitterness, spite
    e. pity, compassion

Questions:

1. Explain Ellen Creighton's problem with the shortage of coffee. Why does Matt send Jethro to Nancy's for coffee when Ellen says she doesn't want any? How does Ellen feel about her craving?

2. What acts of kindness does Jethro extend to Jake Roscoe?

3. Summarize the confrontation between Jethro and Guy Wortman at Gardiner's General Store.

4. How does Ross Milton help Jethro?

5. What does Jethro learn about the fighting at Pittsburg Landing? Why is this of concern to him?

Thinking About the Story:

6. How does the trip to Nancy's for coffee change Jethro's attitude toward John's wife and children? What changes come about in his relationship with her and his nephews as a result?

7. In Chapter 5, find the example of personification describing the Burdow place as Jethro passes it on his way to town. The *mood* of a story is the feeling or emotion an author evokes in the reader through the use of sensory words or phrases. Notice the details Hunt uses to describe the Burdow place. What *mood* is set by this description?

8. *Hyperbole* (hi PER bo lee) is a term meaning extravagant exaggeration. Hyperbole is often used for emphasis, humor, or irony. In Chapter 5, look at Mr. Milton's warning to Jethro about Guy Wortman's love for violence. How does Ross Milton use hyperbole to make his point to Jethro?

9. What does Guy Wortman attempt on Jethro's trip home from Newton? How does Dave Burdow help? Considering his reputation in the community, why might Mr. Burdow have decided to do this?

Dig Deeper:

10. The *theme* of a novel is a main idea or lesson that the author attempts to convey to the reader. One theme in *Across Five Aprils* is the hardships of coming of age. In the last week of March 1862, two significant events occur in Jethro's life: his trip to Newton and the illness of his father. Explain the changes these events bring about in Jethro's life.

11. List three or four other examples in Chapters 5 and 6 that show Jethro's growth from boyhood to manhood.

12. God wants us to grow and mature in our spiritual lives as we grow physically and mentally. Read the following scriptures, then match each area of growth with the passage that teaches it.

a.	_____	1 Corinthians 13:11	1.	Get rid of bad habits, grow in your salvation.
b.	_____	Colossians 1: 9–12	2.	Learn to distinguish good from evil.
c.	_____	1 Peter 2: 1–2	3.	Put away childish things.
d.	_____	Hebrews 5:12–14	4.	Grow in your knowledge of God.

Persuasive Writing Assignment:

Choose one of the biblical elements of growth from question 12 and write three paragraphs explaining why it is a necessary step to being truly mature. Persuasive writing shares your opinion and should convince the reader that you are right.

- Step one is to choose which step of maturity you will write about.
- Step two is to develop your argument. It should be written so that someone can respond in a "yes" or "no" fashion, agree or disagree. For example, a persuasive subject might say: "A necessary step toward adulthood is learning to budget your income." To such a statement the reader can say "Yes, I agree," or "No, I don't agree." A strictly informative statement, such as, "Budgeting for teens," has no position or opinion with which the reader can agree or disagree.
- Step three is to gather details and create an outline. Write down facts and other information that support your subject. For example:
  - Many teenagers need and must buy a car to get to work.
  - Teen expenses may include entertainment, food, gas, insurance, tithe, clothing, gifts, and savings for college.
  - Most teenagers begin work at age 16, yet save little by age 18.

Now outline your paper. For example:

```
I. Teens making money.
   A. Income
   B. Expenses
   C. Savings
```

Your first paragraph should introduce your subject and explain your opinion. Your next paragraph should give supporting details for each item outlined. Your last paragraph should state again your opinion and summarize the details that support it. Write your first draft and have someone read through it and offer advice, if possible. Next rewrite and proofread the new draft. Last, write your final draft, proofread it, and turn in.

Optional Class Discussion Activity:

1. Which of the passages in question 12 speaks to an area where you need growth in your spiritual life? Brainstorm on steps you can take to begin the growth process in each area.

2. Discuss mob violence or vigilantism such as occurred in Chapter 6 with the burning of the Creightons' barn and polluting of their well. Why do some men feel they are above the law? Why do vigilantes or those involved in mob violence rarely want their faces seen or their names known? In what way does Christ ask us to overcome hatred like this? Read Romans 12: 14–21 and Luke 6:7–36 and discuss how they apply to the question.

Chapters 7 & 8

Vocabulary:

Match each vocabulary word with its definition by writing the letter in the blank provided. Some words will not be used.

_____ 1.	occurring or coming after	a. furrow
_____ 2.	cheap trinket or ornament	b. contempt
_____ 3.	lack of ability to perform	c. subsequent
_____ 4.	narrow groove made by a plow	d. zeal
_____ 5.	adorned or enhanced by ornamentation	e. dispel
_____ 6.	eager desire; enthusiasm for a person or cause	f. incompetence
_____ 7.	to drive off; scatter	g. embellished
_____ 8.	to lie hidden, as in ambush	h. proprietor
_____ 9.	owner of a business	i. bauble
_____ 10.	unrelenting, doesn't give up	j. engraved
		k. lurk
		l. tenacious

Questions:

1. What news does Dan Lawrence bring to the Creightons?

2. While studying the names and dates in the family Bible, Jethro learns new information about himself and his family. Name at least three things he learns.

   a.

   b.

   c.

3. How does the news of Tom's death change Jenny's attitude toward her future?

4. How does Sam Gardiner bring a stop to Guy Wortman's troublemaking? How does the community react to this?

5. How does General Beauregard accomplish a southern "victory" at Corinth? What does General Halleck claim about his occupation of the city?

6. How does Dave Burdow help the Creightons rebuild? How does this kindness change community attitude toward the Burdows?

7. ***Connections with History (optional):*** Throughout these two chapters, we learn much about the attitudes of the community toward a number of Civil War generals, both northern and southern. List three or more of the generals, name the significant battles in which they occupied a leadership role, and tell what they

accomplished or failed to accomplish. (Note: Remember to add flags to your map to show the locations of each of these battles.)

		General **Battle**
		Accomplishments/Failures

8. As the war drags on, how do the attitudes of the soldiers and the nation begin to change regarding the President and government of the Union?

9. *Juxtaposition* is the act of placing two things side by side for comparison or contrast. An author uses juxtaposition to underscore the distinctive characteristics of two people, things, happenings, or places. At the end of Chapter 7, what two things does the author juxtapose in the country and the city newspapers? What does this comparison emphasize?

10. A *metaphor* is an implied or stated comparison of two unlike things, but no comparison word (*like* or *as*) is used. For example, "Sherman's march was a raging sea of destruction." In this sentence, Sherman's march is compared to a raging sea by actually *calling* it a raging sea. Underline the metaphor in each of the following passages, then tell what comparison is being made.

    a. Now the cabin had the look of a lonely old man brooding in the summer sunlight.

    ______________________ is compared to ______________________

    b. If they wished to think of him as an ignorant child, he must not try to change their idea of him, but it was a bitter dose to swallow.

    ______________________ is compared to ______________________

Dig Deeper:

11. As the Creighton barn is being rebuilt, one of the men says to Jethro, "Be glad you're a boy, young feller, and don't hev to pester yourself with all these troubles that men be sufferin' through these days." What is Jethro's response to the comment? What do we learn about his inner character from this response?

12. Read 1 Corinthians 13: 4–5, 11. How does Jethro's answer connect with this passage of Scripture? How does his response indicate his growth from childhood toward adulthood?

13. Reread the two letters from Shadrach Yale that the Creightons receive in Chapter 8. What is Shad's opinion of General McClellan? Of General Burnside?

14. Read Titus 3:1–2 and Romans 13:1–7. According to these verses, what should our attitude be regarding those in authority over us? Does Shad have this attitude? Why or why not?

Class Discussion:

In the first of Shadrach's two letters near the end of Chapter 8, he says of General McClellan, "He does not have the cold approach to killing, the singleness of purpose, the brutal tenacity, that the winner of this war—if there ever is to be one—must have." What does Shadrach mean by this? Do you think a Christian can or should be able to act in such a way, even in war? Use scripture in your discussion as much as possible.

As an alternative to this discussion, you may wish to examine and discuss the life and circumstances of one of the great warrior kings of the Old Testament, King David. How can David's obvious skill and pleasure in being a warrior be reconciled with his being "a man after God's own heart" (1 Samuel 13:13, 14; Acts 13:22)?

Chapters 9 & 10

Vocabulary:

A *thesaurus* is a book that is a wonderful tool, giving many synonyms and antonyms of a word. It is an ideal way to expand your vocabulary and find the perfect words to express your ideas most accurately. Use a thesaurus to define each word below, then complete the sentences below, using the correct vocabulary word. You will not use all the words.

1. contempt ________________________
2. desperadoes ________________________
3. draft (military) ________________________
4. forays ________________________
5. impudent ________________________
6. optimism ________________________
7. ridicule ________________________
8. speculation ________________________

a. Until then, he had not thought of his speech as being subject to ____________________.

b. Some men between 20 and 45 years tried to dodge the ____________________ so they wouldn't have to serve in the war.

c. Soldiers held in ____________________ the men who did not serve in the war.

d. Jethro tossed at night wondering if he had done an ____________________ thing.

e. Sometimes soldiers were ____________________ about their new leaders, and sometimes their attitudes were pessimistic, especially after a loss.

Questions:

1. Define what a deserter is, and describe Point Prospect campground after the deserters arrive.

2. How does the presence of the deserters change everyday life for the Creighton family?

3. If an eligible man did not wish to serve in the army, how could he avoid going?

4. What is Jethro's family supposed to do if Eb Carron shows up? What are the possible consequences if they don't?

5. What happens to Shadrach Yale at the Battle of Gettysburg? How is he found by his family?

6. What convinces Matt Creighton to allow Jenny to go to Washington?

7. What is Jethro's response to the news of Shadrach's injury?

8. Explain how Jenny helps the wounded soldiers.

Thinking About the Story:

9. In Chapter 9, as Eb talks with Jethro by the field, Eb says, "I was an awful fool—at least you got a chancet in battle—maybe it's one in a hundred, but it's a chancet. This way, I got none." What does he mean? Why are Eb and the deserters in Point Prospect so desperate and hopeless?

10. After Eb reveals himself to Jethro, Jethro begins to realize that some situations are not nearly as black or white, right or wrong, as we might think. The law says one thing, his heart says another, and family and friends may well have different opinions on what is right. To try to figure things out, Jethro begins to weigh in his mind the consequences of turning Eb in or letting him go free. In the two columns below, write down the things Jethro considers that support each action.

Turn Eb In	Let Eb Go Free

11. Irony comes in several forms in literature. In general *irony* is a difference between appearance and reality, or between what is expected and what actually happens. *Dramatic irony* is when the reader sees a character's mistakes which the character is unable to see himself. With *verbal irony,* the author or character says one thing but means something entirely different. Explain what kind of irony the following quote contains and why it is ironic when Jethro says,

> And what was it that man said the day of the barn-raisin'? "It's good that you're a boy and don't have to worry yourself about this war." Why yes, no doubt about it, eleven-year-old boys ain't got a thing to worry about; this year of 1863 is a fine, carefree time for eleven-year-old boys. . . .

Dig Deeper:

12. Jethro's effort to keep Eb hidden and secret creates stress for him personally and in his relationship with his sister. Was it right to make these decisions and take these risks on his own at age 11? Why or why not?

13. Read Proverbs 15:22, 17:17, 20:18, and Luke 14:28–30. What can these verses teach us? Summarize them and explain how these verses could have affected Jethro's decision.

14. Lincoln writes to Jethro saying, "you will understand when I say if it be a wrong one [decision], then I have erred on the side of mercy." What does this mercy mean to Eb? Read James 2:13 and Matthew 18:21–35. What do these verses teach us about being merciful? In what way did Lincoln's decision to forgive deserters reflect this?

15. Both Jethro and Jenny take on burdens and responsibilities that normally would be beyond their years. Why do you think Jenny was allowed to marry? Do you think they were mature enough to do the things they did? Why or why not?

Optional Activities and Class Discussions:

1. Was Jethro right in "going over the heads" of the Federal registrars in appealing to President Lincoln on behalf of the deserters? Why or why not? Who in the country had ultimate authority? Consider Acts 25:1–12.

2. Read the Biblical account of the friendship of Jonathan and David in 1 Samuel 20:1–42, as well as Jesus' words to the Pharisees, who tried to trap him, in Matthew 22:15–22. What do these passages have to say about obedience to the laws of the land? Is it right for a Christian to take a stand against a law or authority? If so, under what circumstances? If not, why not?

3. In a class discussion or short paper, discuss the meaning of "submission." Does submission always mean obedience, or does submission sometimes mean disobedience but acceptance of the consequences without complaint or challenge? Review Acts 4:1–20, 25:1–12; Romans 13:1–7; Hebrews 13:17; 1 Peter 2:13–23, and use them in your discussion.

Connections With History:

4. Chapter 10 includes vast amounts of information about the Civil War in 1863. Complete the list below, naming the location of each battle. (Optionally, you may also research the battle outcomes and victors. You may consult outside resources to complete any data omitted in the novel.) Note: Remember to add flags to your map at the locations of these battles.

Civil War Battles of 1863

Generals	*Battle Location*	*Outcomes/Victors*
Hooker vs. Lee		
Rosecrans vs. Bragg		
Grant vs. Pemberton		
Meade vs. Lee		

Chapters 11 & 12

Vocabulary:

Next to each phrase below, write the word from the Word List that most closely matches the definition, then write a sentence using that word.

Word List

amnesty	annals	complicity	irreparable	jubilation
obscurity	paeans	pandemonium	tranquil	vindictiveness

1. unable to be mended or repaired ______________________
   Sentence:

2. partnership in wrongdoing; being an accomplice ______________________
   Sentence:

3. a state of uncertainty; a lack of clarity ______________________
   Sentence:

4. historical records; reports ______________________
   Sentence:

5. disorder; chaos; wild lawlessness ______________________
   Sentence:

6. quiet; calm; free of commotion ______________________
   Sentence:

7. a spirit of revenge ______________________
   Sentence:

8. a feeling of joy; an act of celebration ______________________
   Sentence:

9. songs of praise or thanksgiving; hymns ______________________
   Sentence:

10. a general pardon for offenses against a government ______________________
    Sentence:

Questions:

1. What new information does Jethro learn about the Battle of Chickamauga?

2. What were some of the reactions that people had to Lincoln's "Gettysburg Address"?

3. Who were the political candidates for the office of President of the United States in the election of 1864? State each one's position on dealings with the Confederate states.

4. How did Matt Creighton's neighbors react to Sherman's march?

Thinking About the Story:

5. What were the provisions of Lincoln's proclamation of amnesty?

6. What is Jethro's reaction to the amnesty?

7. Explain Ross Milton's fears of Congress's passing the 13th Amendment of the Constitution.

8. Compare Ross Milton's comments about abolitionists' attitudes toward freed slaves with the statements Wilse Graham had made earlier. What concerns do both men share?

9. Describe the reunion of John and Bill. What information does Bill want Ma to know? How do you think the family feels when they learn this?

10. Each passage below contains either a metaphor or personification. Underline the descriptive phrase in the sentence and in the blank provided write an M for metaphor or a P for personification.

    a. _____ "But his face was full of light as the crowds cheered. . . ."
    b. _____ "When it comes to the final vote, the country will not admit that its sons have died for nothing."
    c. _____ "Don't expect peace to be a perfect pearl, Jeth.'"
    d. _____ ". . . the fifth April had become, like her four older sisters, a time of grief and desolation."
    e. _____ ". . . the soft golden blanket of sunlight over the fields and orchards seemed out of place—like laughter in a church."

11. Remember that juxtaposition is the act of placing two things side by side for comparison or contrast. An author uses juxtaposition to underscore the distinctive characteristics of two people, things, happenings, or places. *Antithesis* on the other hand, contrasts ideas and words in parallel sentence structure. The author will present an idea or image, and then in parallel phrasing present the opposite idea or image. For example:

    "Give me liberty or give me death."—Patrick Henry

    "One small step for a man, one giant leap for mankind."—Neil Armstrong

    Underline the antithesis in each selection below.

    a. "There was no time or opportunity to go to Springfield, no hope of looking upon a face at once the plainest and the most beautiful, the humblest and the most magnificent, that Jethro would know in his lifetime."

b. "He had not embraced one of his brothers since the days of his very early childhood, but that morning he put his arms about Shadrach, and slowly the joy for the living assuaged a little the grief for the dead."

12. How does Ed Turner's son, Sammy, describe Sherman's march and looting of the south? What is Ed Turner afraid his son will learn?

13. Ross Milton warns Jethro that peace will not be a perfect pearl or a shining dream. What are Ross Milton's reasons for this statement?

14. Where do Ross Milton and Jethro put their hope for real peace? What is the country's and Jeth's reaction when Lincoln is killed?

15. Why does Ross Milton call the 13th Amendment abolishing slavery only "a dim pinpoint of light in the darkness"?

Dig Deeper:

16. Early in Chapter 12, the author begins describing Sherman's "march through Georgia" by quoting people's reactions to it, by describing it in a letter from Ed Turner's son, and in a discussion between Turner and Matt Creighton. Reread

those pages and then *paraphrase* (simplify and explain in your own words) what Sherman's army did on its march through Georgia.

17. Also early in Chapter 12, before Irene Hung begins to describe Sherman's march through Georgia, in a paragraph that begins "Then during the next weeks, stories about Sherman's march began filtering back," the author begins to describe the homes and situations in the Midwest. Why do you think the author describes the Midwest before she describes the destruction of Sherman's march through the South? What literary term describes what the author does here? Is it effective?

18. President Lincoln told Jethro in his letter that "if I err it will be on the side of mercy," which he demonstrated both in his amnesty for the deserters and his proclamation of amnesty for the southern states. Read Psalm 103: 8–10, Luke 6: 27–36, Romans 12:18, Colossians 3:12–15, 1 Peter 3:8–12. What do these verses teach us about true mercy, forgiveness, and peace?

Optional Activities:

1. *Class Discussion:* Read Lincoln's famous "Gettysburg Address" in an encyclopedia or other reference. Read the speech in class, then discuss the purpose of the speech. What is your opinion of the speech? How do you think Lincoln's audience might have responded to it?

2. Research the surrender of Robert E. Lee at Appomattox Court House and write a one- to three-paragraph summary of the events.

3 Read about the assassination of Abraham Lincoln. Prepare a two- to four-minute speech or write a two- to five-paragraph expository paper about the assassination.

4. When President Lincoln was killed, the author writes "People would ask for many years: 'Where were you when you heard? What were you doing? Who brought you the word?'" Often, learning of terrible or shocking news can burn that instant into our memory. For more recent generations, similar events have been the bombing of Pearl Harbor, the ending of World War II, the assassination of President John F. Kennedy, and the attacks on the World Trade Center and the Pentagon on September 11, 2001. Sometimes it can be more personal, such as the death or injury of a friend or family member. Have you had a moment such as this? In a few paragraphs or a poem, tell what happened and your feelings about it.

Overview

1. The *plot* of a novel is the series of interconnected events that take place in a narrative. These events are connected by the novel's *conflict*—the struggle between opposing forces. In a few sentences, sum up the conflict in *Across Five Aprils.*

2. The complications that occur as a novel progresses toward its climax are known as the *rising action.* These complications are usually connected to the main conflict, causing speculation about the outcome of the conflict. What complications form the *rising action* of *Across Five Aprils*?

3. The peak and pivotal point of the conflict, the moment one discovers the outcome of the action, is called the *climax.* It is the turning point of the story and sets in motion the eventual conclusion of the plot's central conflict. What is the climax of *Across Five Aprils*?

4. In the *resolution* or *denouement* (day noo MAH) of a story, all plot complications are finally sorted out, the conflict is solved, and the story is brought to a conclusion. What is the resolution of *Across Five Aprils?*

5. Every story has a conflict, or problem, to be solved by the main character or characters. The following are common forms of conflict:

   - **Man vs. Man:** Characters struggle against each other.
   - **Man vs. Himself:** Characters' struggle is internal—a struggle against character flaws, for example.
   - **Man vs. Nature:** Characters struggle for survival against the forces of nature.
   - **Man vs. Society:** Characters struggle against social rules or laws, usually shown as unjust.
   - **Man vs. God:** Characters struggle against God.

   Which of these forms of conflict best describes the conflict in *Across Five Aprils*? Why?

6. A *motif* is a recurring image, object, or idea in a novel. Motifs act as unifying devices in literature and often are related to a novel's theme. There is one obvious motif in *Across Five Aprils*—the month of April, as named in the title. How does the author use the month of April to communicate one of the novel's major themes? Who grows and changes like the seasons? Explain why you think so.

7. Another motif in the story is disillusionment—one Union general after another seems to offer success, only to fail. Even President Lincoln fails in the end to lead the nation through recovery because he is murdered. Read Psalm 20:7, 118:8–9; Daniel 3:14–18; Romans 8:28, 33–39. According to these scriptures, in whom should we put our trust and faith in bad times? Who has the ability to save and keep us?

Essay and Writing Suggestions

1. *Creative writing project:*
   a. Write an original short story about someone during wartime, using the techniques of simile, metaphor, personification, and others that you have learned about in this guide.
   b. Write a sequel to the story. What happens to Jethro as he goes to school and lives with Shad and Jenny? What does the future hold for him? Or write about Bill being released from prison camp and what happens as he returns home.

2. *Essay:* Is the damage caused by the local troublemakers (Guy Wortman and his followers) different from the damage caused by the Civil War armies? Consider their motivations for doing what they do. What does each desire? Do they essentially seek the same ends or do they not? Compose your thoughts in a one- to two-page essay.

3. *Essay:* What universal truth(s) do you find in this story? Write a three- to five-page essay on why it is important, in what ways it affects your life and your family, how it affects society around you, and in what way life would improve for society and your country if more people followed this truth. You may also wish to include any ideas you have for encouraging the active growth of this truth in yourself and the people around you.

4. *Civil War Letters:* Study a specific battle of the Civil War. Write an imaginary letter from a soldier, nurse, or observer to his or her parents or family at home. You could write letters home from the same battlefield by both a Confederate and a Union soldier. Some family members may have copies of actual Civil War letters for you to use as a model.

5. *Biographies*: There were many fascinating people connected with the Civil War. Abraham Lincoln, Jefferson Davis, Frederick Douglass, Harriet Tubman, William Lloyd Garrison, John Wilkes Booth, Robert E. Lee, Ulysses S. Grant, Stonewall Jackson, William Sherman, Stephen A. Douglas, and John Brown, just to name a few. Find a few good books in the library about one of these people and write a biography of that person.

6. *Field Trip:* There are literally hundreds of Civil War battlefields in the United States: Gettysburg, Bull Run (Manassas), Chancellorsville, Antietam, etc. It may be possible for you to pay a visit to one of these battlefields. Before your visit, spend some time studying the particulars of the battle that took place there. Keep a journal and/or photographic record of your trip.

7. Though you may not live near a Civil War battlefield, most communities in states and territories of the time sent troops to the war. Do a paper or presentation on the troops who went from your community. Where did they train and fight? What were their experiences? Check with a local museum or historical society for resources and information.

8. To write a theme paper, choose a theme from the book, explain it, and support your opinion with examples and ideas from the book. Your opening paragraph should state your main point and grab your reader's attention. The body should use examples to express the main points you wish to make. The closing paragraph should tie the paper together, restating your main point in a new way.

   a. Write a one- to two-page theme paper focusing on the theme of "mercy" as defined by characters in *Across Five Aprils*. Analyze ways in which many of the characters showed mercy.

   b. Write a one- to two-page theme paper focusing on the theme of "forgiveness" as experienced by the characters in *Across Five Aprils*. You may wish to include dictionary definitions as well as synonyms and antonyms and character definitions and examples from the book.

9. Often, the quietest and the humblest person turns out to have more influence than you ever would expect. In what way is Jethro like this? What did this young boy accomplish that was more than you'd ever expect? Write a two- to three-page paper describing him and the way he dramatically changed things for more than one person.

Additional Resources

You may find additional extension activities, projects, and information on this and other Progeny Press titles at `https://www.pinterest.com/progenypress/boards/`.

Other Books by Irene Hunt:

No Promises in the Wind
Up a Road Slowly
The Lottery Rose (a haunting but hopeful book of a young boy recovering from parental abuse.)

Books of Related Interest:

Fiction:

Red Badge of Courage by Stephen Crane
Pink and Say by Patricia Polacco
Red Cap by G. Clifton Wisler
Mr. Lincoln's Drummer by G. Clifton Wisler
Bull Run by Paul Fleischman
Behind Rebel Lines: The Incredible Story of Emma Edmonds, Civil War Spy by Seymour Reit
Shades of Gray by Carolyn Reeder

Nonfiction:

The Boys' War: Confederate and Union Soldiers Talk About the Civil War by Jim Murphy
Lincoln: A Photobiography by Russell Freedman
Civil War Sites: The Official Guide to Battlefields, Monuments, and More by Civil War Preservation Trust

Website and Documentary

`http://www.pbs.org/kenburns/civil-war/`
This website is for the documentary series *The Civil War,* by Ken Burns, done for PBS, an excellent resource.

Answer Key

Note: Most of the questions in Progeny Press study guides deal with students' understanding and interpretation of issues in the novel; therefore, most answers will be individual to the student. Progeny Press answer keys are designed to be as inclusive as possible for the teacher and/or parent, giving enough background and information to judge whether the student has grasped the essence of the issue and the question. We try to point out some directions students' answers might take, which directions might be best, and some errors that may appear. Students are not expected to answer as completely as the answers provided in the Answer Key.

Ideas for Prereading Activities

The answers given below are for teachers' reference and are not answers, per se.

1. The economies of the northern and southern states led to stress between the two groups. While the South was largely agricultural-based and believed it needed slave labor to maintain its economy, the North had many more cities and factories and relied on cheap immigrant labor. The southern plantations also produced primarily cash crops such as cotton and tobacco, but the northern farms were more diversified and could feed the northern cities. The North also had more railroads and canals to move products. In the event of war, the North was capable of producing many of the military supplies that would be needed to support an army through its factories and also had large numbers of immigrants, providing a pool of workers to replace those who would be removed to support the war efforts. Of course, a major issue dividing the nation was slavery. The southern economy, dependent on huge plantations, was supported by slave labor, and many southerners felt their economy would collapse without this system. Many northerners felt slavery was unconscionable and should be abolished. With much of the economic wealth and power centered in the north, the southern states felt they were being dictated to and forced to follow national laws they believed were pushed on them by the North. The southern states, full of farmers who knew how to use a gun, felt they could "wear down" the northern states with their "weak" city dwellers within the first few months of battle. The north often derided the southerners as "ignorant."

2. *Missouri Compromise:* As the Missouri Territory expanded and desired admission to the United States as a state, the question arose as to whether it should be a free or slave state. When Alabama became a state in 1819, the number of representatives in the Senate from slave and free states was equal. By admitting Maine as a free state and Missouri as a slave state, that equality could be maintained. However, the House of Representatives approved an amendment by James Tallmadge of New York forbidding the importation of slaves and providing for the emancipation of all slaves born in Missouri. The amendment set off a huge debate in the Senate. This led to the compromise of 1820, allowing for Missouri to be admitted as a slave state, but prohibiting slavery in the Louisiana Purchase north of 36°30'N latitude, which is the southern boundary of Missouri. *Kansas-Nebraska Act:* As expansion continued, a bill in 1854 established the territories of Kansas and Nebraska. According to provisions of the Missouri Compromise, slavery should have been prohibited in both. However, proslavery congressmen did not want to see another free territory west of Missouri. Stephen A. Douglas, chairman of the Senate Committee on Territories, introduced legislation specifically repealing the Missouri Compromise, stating that territories should be able to decide the question of slavery themselves (the principle of popular sovereignty). Antislavery forces were enraged, touching off a bitter three-month debate in Congress, but the measure was finally approved, moving the United States much closer to the Civil War. *Dred Scott Case:* Dred Scott was a black slave who was taken by his owners from Missouri, a slave state, to Illinois, a free state, and then to the Wisconsin territory, where slavery was prohibited. Scott appealed to the courts for his freedom. After Scott's freedom was denied by a variety of lower courts, the case went to the U.S. Supreme Court in 1856–57. The decision was made that Scott would remain a slave, and that a black whose ancestors had been slaves was not entitled to the rights of a citizen; therefore Scott had no standing in court. The justices further stated that Congress had no power to prohibit slavery in the territories and that the Missouri Compromise was unconstitutional. The court's decision further divided the northern and southern states. (Scott was later granted his freedom, after being returned to a previous owner; he died in 1858.)

3. The following states seceded from the Union and became the Confederate states: South Carolina, Mississippi, Florida, Alabama, Georgia, Louisiana, Texas, Virginia, Arkansas, Tennessee, and North Carolina. The states that remained in the Union were Maine, New Hampshire, Vermont, Massachusetts, Connecticut, New York, New Jersey, Delaware, Maryland, Pennsylvania, Ohio, Kentucky, Michigan, Indiana, Wisconsin, Illinois, Minnesota, Iowa, Missouri, Oregon,

and California. The "border states" were Delaware, Maryland, Kentucky, and Missouri. They had ties to both North and South, and slavery existed in all four. The effort to maintain their loyalty to the North caused Lincoln much distress during the war. West Virginia was admitted to the Union during this period as a free state.

Chapters 1 & 2
Vocabulary:
Section 1
1. Calvinism: The system of beliefs espoused by John Calvin, based largely on the sovereignty of God.
2. abolitionist: A person who wants to do away with slavery.
3. tariff: Taxes imposed on the shipping of imports and exports.
4. secede: To withdraw from a group or union, generally from a unit of government.

Section 2
5. perplexities: confusions, uncertainties
6. hoisted: lifted upwards
7. strident: having a harsh sound; grating
8. typhoid fever: infectious and often fatal disease, caused by bacteria, resulting in inflamed and ulcerated intestines
9. preoccupation: absorbed, engrossed, thoughts are elsewhere; occupied by something else

Questions:
1. The time setting of the novel at the beginning is mid-April of 1861; warm, springtime weather. The place is the southern Illinois farm of the Creighton family, consisting of a small cabin, barnlot, half-acre potato field, a large field beyond a creek, and an apple orchard.
2. Copernicus was an astronomer who believed the sun is the center of the solar system—prior to his teachings, it was believed that Earth was the center. Jethro introduces the subject of Copernicus' teachings to distract his mother's thinking about war and the death of her young children. Although Ellen questions whether the teachings are biblical, she is proud of Jethro's understanding of things she knows nothing about and is thankful, momentarily, that he has distracted her from her sadness.
3. Jethro thinks the idea of war is exciting because war means banners and bunting, parades of horses and brass bands. Everyone Jethro knows that has ever been involved in a war has survived, so he is not afraid of family members being killed. Those who have actually died seem merely shadows of men from faraway lands.
4. Mary Creighton went to a dance in Hidalgo with Rob Nelson in 1859. A crowd of ruffians come uninvited to the dance, waving whiskey bottles and shouting insults at the guests. As Rob and Mary leave in their wagon, Travis Burdow followed them on horseback. He fired a pistol over the heads of the horses, which frightened them so that they bolted through a rail fence, overturning the wagon. Mary was crushed beneath the wagon.
5. Jethro's love for Bill stems from Bill's calm and quiet disposition. Bill treats people and animals gently; he values education; he is physically strong and a hard worker. He treats Jethro with both kindness and appreciation for his hard work in the fields.
6. Although John and Bill care for each other deeply and seemed to understand each other well, Jethro is ambivalent toward John. Nancy is very shy, which Jethro interprets as being unfriendly, so it makes him uneasy to be around Nancy and her children. He seldom visits John's cabin, even though it is only half a mile from his own.
7. The Civil War begins with the South firing on Fort Sumter, South Carolina. Anderson's men are starving and President Lincoln informs Governor Pickens that he is sending supplies to the fort. General Beauregard demands that the North surrender the fort. When Anderson refuses, Beauregard fires on the fort.

Thinking About the Story:

8. Ellen Creighton cherishes her youngest son Jethro and overlooks behaviors in him for which she would have punished her other children. She feels he is special because he survived the sickness that took three of her other children, and she watches over him with tenderness. She looks up to him for his "book knowledge" and is often amazed at the things he understands at his tender age.
9. As a field worker at the age of 9, Jethro is extended the courtesy of being allowed to eat dinner at the adult table. Coffee is considered "for adults only." When Bill dipped a crust of bread in his coffee and offered it to Jethro, it showed he understood Jethro's movement toward adulthood by taking on the work of planting. Jethro considers the action a favor, but chooses not to draw the attention of the other adults at the table.

10. Wilse Graham is a southerner at heart and defends the South's position on slavery. The South wants the right to live as it sees fit, without interference from the North, he says. He believes England will come to the aid of the South if there is a war, to protect the cotton needed to run the English looms. He also feels northerners will hesitate to welcome the freed, uneducated slaves when the war is over. John questions the right of people to own the souls and bodies of other human beings. Bill states that he hates slavery and says it is greed that motivates slave owners. Matt Creighton responds that human nature is taking on an attitude of decency and responsibility, which is a change from previous history. Ellen is upset by the talk of war, and wants no more of it at the family dinner table.
11. a. like the soldiers of Herod. child's paralysis is compared to Herod's army
b. riding like kings; held high like horses with short reins; men riding are compared to kings; foot soldiers (lesser men in perfect lines) are compared to horses with heads reined up high.
c. pleasant as the sound of a little bell ringing; Jenny's voice is compared to a bell
d. extending like giant claws; tree roots are compared to claws
e. looking somewhat like a solemn dwarf; Jethro is compared to a solemn dwarf
f. like a woman talkin' to a young 'un; Bill's speech to his horse is compared to a woman's speech to a child.
Idioms:
12. Taking away someone's enthusiasm.
13. Someone cannot criticize another for a fault they have themselves.
14. A very old saying that means you'd endure terrible hardships for someone else because of your love for them.
15. Saying different things to different people about the same subject.
16. To change ones' mind, to vacillate. Unable to decide what they really want to do.
Dig Deeper:
17. The grandfather of Travis Burdow had been accused of stealing a team of horses and had fled to Jasper County to escape prosecution. Because of this, an air of suspicion and dislike has settled on the family, causing his children to be persecuted. His son Dave is sullen and silent and keeps to himself. His children (including Travis) are often the same, but are given to drunkenness, which gives them courage and increases their defiance. The author states that the gunshot fired over the heads of Rob Nelson's horses was "fired at a society that had kicked a boy from childhood on because he bore his grandfather's name."
18. Jethro finds it difficult to accept that Travis Burdow paid no consequences for the actions that led to Mary's death. This reminds him of Lincoln's wavering regarding the declaration of war, and Jethro finds himself angry at both his father's actions and Lincoln's inaction. Jethro wonders if it is the fear of having "blood on people's hands" which motivates both men.
19. Answers will vary. Matthew Creighton's actions are godly in that he was slow to anger and showed compassion to those who had wronged his family. He chose to repay an evil act with one of kindness. He could not quite go so far as to show love for the Burdows, however. As God has not dealt with us as our sins deserve, so Matthew did not deal with Travis Burdow as his sin deserved.
20. Answers will vary. Ezekiel 18 tells us that God will not hold a grudge against a son who lives righteously, despite the sins of his father. Each soul will be judged based on their own guilt or righteousness. Although the community never punished any of the Burdows in a legal sense, they never trusted them and they made them outcasts because of the grandfather's actions.
21. Ellen's religious upbringing taught her to depend on the sovereignty of God, and did not allow her to regret her own fading beauty. She's lived a hard life, losing four of her twelve children. Sickness and poverty taught her that a pretty face is of little value when it comes to survival.
22. Answers will vary. Matthew Creighton's intervention teaches us that he is not afraid to stand up for what he believes is right. He is not vengeful, even in grief. He obviously is well respected by the community and exercises great influence over his neighbors. He is able to persuade them to put aside their revenge and thereby avoid further bloodshed and death.

Chapters 3 & 4
Connections to History:
1. *Jefferson Davis:* President of the Confederate States. Davis served as U.S. Senator from Missouri until that state seceded from the Union in 1861. He left his Senate seat and was elected to command the state's military forces. However, within a few weeks he was elected President of the Confederate States. *Robert E. Lee:* Military general and

genius of the South. He was originally approached by Lincoln to lead northern troops, but declined in favor of the southern command. Much of the southern successes were due to Lee's military expertise. *Ulysses S. Grant:* Northern military general. He was sometimes a great disappointment as a military leader, as he proved ineffective and indecisive in several battles. However, he pursued Lee's forces at Richmond and Petersburg for 10 months, finally forcing the surrender of Lee's Army of Northern Virginia at Appomattox on April 9, 1865. In 1868, Grant was elected President of the United States. *George Meade:* Northern general. After serving at Bull Run and Antietam, Meade broke through Confederate troops at Fredericksburg and Chancellorsville, Virginia, but was unable to succeed in victory because of the late arrival of supporting troops. Three days before the Battle of Gettysburg, he was given command and succeeded in winning this pivotal battle for the North. *William Tecumseh Sherman:* Northern military leader responsible for the "march to the sea," in which a large portion of Georgia was annihilated. His troops tore up railroads, released slaves, and burned plantations along the way. Sherman presented the city of Savannah to President Lincoln as a Christmas gift, then proceeded toward South Carolina, where he continued the destruction. Charleston and Columbia both fell to northern control. The South was unable to make a comeback after his sweeping attack. *Abraham Lincoln:* 16th President of the United States. Lincoln desired to "preserve the Union" at all cost. He suffered much criticism on the part of both sides—from the North, because of his inability to appoint a strong military leader; and from the South, because of his personal stand against slavery. He was assassinated by John Wilkes Booth prior to the end of the Civil War.

3. *Bull Run:* Brigadier General Irvin McDowell was defeated by the Confederates and subsequently relieved of command and replaced by McClellan. Thomas J. Jackson earned his nickname, "Stonewall," at this battle. This battle let the North know that the war would not be over quickly and the southern forces would not be taken easily. *Fort Henry and Fort Donelson:* Ulysses S. Grant captured Fort Henry in Tennessee on Feb. 6, 1862, and 10 days later captured Fort Donelson. As a result, the South was forced to give up Kentucky and parts of Tennessee. They would later retrench and meet the Union forces at Shiloh.

Vocabulary:

1. prestige; 2. resolve; 3. fiasco; 4. blithely; 5. bunting; 6. quavering; 7. nullify; 8. sullen; 9. emancipator; 10. oratory; 11. denounce; 12. wastrel

Questions:

1. The Mason-Dixon line formed the boundary between Pennsylvania and Maryland. It was commonly regarded as the dividing line between the North and the South.
2. Tom and Eb leave first. They join the northern side, the Union.
3. Frémont is praised for taking a stand against slavery; but he is also criticized for creating turmoil in Missouri by emancipating slaves there.
4. Jethro has nightmares about the war. When he awakes, Bill is often sitting beside him on the bed, talking quietly to comfort him.
5. Matt Creighton overheard Jethro talking to his deceased older siblings as if they were still alive. Jethro's father may have felt this wasn't healthy for Jethro.
6. Bells are rung at the fall of Fort Henry in Tennessee and at the fall of Fort Donnelson. General Ulysses S. Grant is credited with both victories.
7. General Buckner requests terms of peace, but Grant replies that only "an unconditional and immediate surrender can be accepted."

Thinking About the Story:

8. People in the North generally believed the war would be won swiftly by the North. Early southern victories convinced them that it would instead be a long and difficult war to win.
9. While talking with Bill, Jethro realizes his brother is no longer having a conversation, but is thinking aloud about the war. Jethro realizes he will soon be alone. Bill feels that hatred has caused the war and that nobody ever truly wins. In his eyes, slave owners and factory owners are equally responsible for the institution of slavery, as both enjoy wealth from it. Bill does not want to see the nation split, but he believes that abolishing slavery will ruin the South's economy and that the North should not be able to tell the South what to do.
10. It is hot on the way to Fort Donelson, and many soldiers cast off their winter clothes and heavy blankets. Many soldiers later freeze to death. Tom was not as proud of the Union victory as he might have been, knowing that many soldiers died because of their own foolishness.

11. "Oak, maple, and poplar; sumac, wild-grape, and dogwood—they all smiled at him . . . and they said, 'What war, little boy, what war?'" Hunt describes the trees on the hill as smiling at Jethro and talking to him.
12. "Somewhere, far off in another field a man shouted to his horses, and the shout died away in a cry that ran frightened over the brown water of the creek and into the darkening woods."
13. a. Answers may vary, but should mention that something is going to cause wailing and grief, something may happen to Bill.
b. Answers may vary but should mention that hard, sad things are coming, and Jethro will face grief that will tear him apart. Jethro will do a lot of growing up in a short time.
14. The North wanted to control access to the Tennessee and Cumberland Rivers in Kentucky, as well as to the railroad, in order to cut off supplies to the southern forts. Control of the Mississippi River would, in essence, cut the Confederacy in two, assuring a Union victory.
15. The sadness and reality of Mary's death is the first change. Then he is on Walnut Hill when he learns of the fight between John and Bill and that Bill is now leaving for the war. The familiar sounds of the area now resemble a wail or crying.
16. Shad rebukes Jethro because Shad feels the office of president deserves the respect of the people, even though many people call President Lincoln by much worse names than "Ol' Abe." Lincoln is criticized by the southerners for his stand on slavery; he is criticized by the northerners for his apparent lack of leadership and his choice of weak generals. His looks, his speech patterns, and his family also are all objects of criticism. However, some people sympathize with him and his family over the death of his son Willie. Answers will vary, but probably Jethro heard the nickname often and thought of it as a friendly nickname rather than a derogatory nickname. He decides to never use it again.
Dig Deeper:
17. Answers will vary. The verse is telling us that a person's sincerity or confidence in his own actions does not necessarily mean that he is doing the right thing. Subjectively, or from our point of view, things may seem clear, but someone with a more objective point of view, someone who can see more than we can, might see how wrong we are. All of the Creighton brothers believe they are doing the right thing, but they cannot all be right. In fact, some of them may be doing the right thing for the wrong reasons, or the wrong thing for the right reasons. Bill is at least sensitive enough to realize that he may be wrong, and he realizes that neither the North or the South is fully in the right. Personal applications of this verse will vary. One hopes this verse makes us stop and review our own attitudes and the things we accept as right, because the verse specifically says the way "*seems right* to a man" but it "leads to death." We should be humble in our opinions and always recognize that we may be wrong. It also should lead us to take all our concerns and questions to the Bible, the Word of God, not man.
18. Answers will vary, but should mention that Jethro accepted the cold as part of his lot in life, just as he accepted the need to help out on the farm or take over the chores for his brothers. The cold was a "necessary evil" to endure to enjoy Shad's company, the warmth of a fire, and the fresh bread he was carrying to share with Shad.
19. James writes that the testing of our faith develops perseverance or patience, which leads to maturity. We are also promised wisdom from God, if we ask.

Chapters 5 & 6
Vocabulary:
1. c, 2. a, 3. b, 4. c, 5. e, 6. d, 7. c, 8. b, 9. a, 10. d, 11. e, 12. b
Questions:
1. If Ellen Creighton does not drink coffee, she suffers from migraine headaches. Matt understands her condition and sends Jethro to borrow coffee because he does not like to see her suffer needlessly. Ellen, however, feels her dependency is a weakness—an evil hold on her—and she feels powerless to overcome it.
2. Jethro takes time to visit with Jake Roscoe and to answer his questions about the war. He also purchases a newspaper for him while he is in Newton.
3. Answers will vary, but may mention some of the following. Jethro is questioned by Guy Wortman as to the whereabouts of his brother Bill. When Jethro answers that the family has not heard from him, Wortman makes it clear that he and others in the community are unhappy about Bill's southern sympathies. He also threatens harm to Jethro's father. Ross Milton reminds Wortman that Matt's other sons are fighting for the Union, but that does not satisfy Wortman.

Guy challenges Jethro further, asking if his father taught him that Bill deserves to be shot as a traitor. Jethro replies that he thinks quite highly of his brother and his father doesn't teach him one way or another. Wortman becomes furious and stalks out.

4. Ross Milton verbally defends Matt Creighton and Jethro in the confrontation with Guy Wortman. He purchases dinner for Jethro and arranges for his horse to be cared for. Then he gives Jethro a grammar book.

5. The Union won the battle at Pittsburg Landing, but more than 20,000 men died; 12,000 of whom were from the North. It concerns Jethro that Tom and Eb may have been in it and may have been hurt or killed.

Thinking About the Story:

6. Nancy speaks about her and her children's loneliness for John. When Jethro tries to respond, he's unable to find the right words, but feels great sympathy for her. He has always shied away from the children, but now takes the time to pat their heads. Later when she visits him while he is plowing, they talk comfortably, and he heeds Nancy's wisdom regarding the letter Jenny received from Shad. He begins to develop a relationship with Nancy's boys.

7. The personification is "as if some evil lay close to the ground on its belly and peered out at him." Answers about mood may vary, but should mention something like: Irene Hunt sets a mood that is dark, threatening, almost palpably alive in its evil intent. It invokes a sense of fear and dread.

8. Ross Milton says that Guy Wortman loves violence so much that he would join a mob, even if it was to murder his own grandmother. This is probably not true, but it emphasizes how dangerous a man Guy Wortman is.

9. A drunken Guy Wortman runs alongside Jethro's team, whipping them across their backs, hoping to cause the wagon to overturn. Dave Burdow had overheard Wortman's intentions to cause harm, boarded Jethro's wagon in the woods, and took over the reins. He is able to keep the horses under control. Answers may vary, but may mention Burdow's feeling of indebtedness to Jethro's father for persuading the community to not lynch his son, Travis, after the death of Mary. They also may mention that he felt partially responsible for his sons' actions and didn't want Matt Creighton to lose another child when this time he could do something to prevent it, or that he simply is better than many people give him credit for and he did not want to see Jethro harmed.

Dig Deeper:

10. The trip to Newton gives Jethro the opportunity to accomplish an adult's job on his own. He manages the team of horses, makes the required purchases, and stands up to the accusations of Guy Wortman. The illness of his father requires Jethro to take over the day-to-day operations of the farm on his own. He now must be concerned with the weather, the harvest, and whether there will be sufficient food for his family and the animals. Jethro is taking on the responsibilities of an adult.

11. Answers will vary, but may include: Jethro's relationship with Jenny is changing—he changes in relationship from a little brother to a peer. When she receives a letter from Shad and doesn't want to share it entirely with the family, Jethro is irritated; however, he accepts correction over this from Nancy. Jethro's relationship with Nancy and her children is also changing to a more responsible and caring older uncle. He works hard on the farm to provide a living for John's family as well as his own. Jethro is beginning to understand the need for improving his speech and grammar. He diligently reads the newspapers and studies the war effort. He is discriminating in his decisions of what information to share with his parents about the war.

12. a. 3, b. 4, c. 1, d. 2.

Chapters 7 & 8

Vocabulary:

1. c; 2. i; 3. f; 4. a; 5. g; 6. d; 7. e; 8. k; 9. h; 10. l

Questions:

1. Dan Lawrence tells the Creightons of the death of Tom. He describes the battle and explains that he was with Tom when he died and tells them that Tom did not suffer.

2. Answers will vary, but should include three of the following: Jethro learns that the older children fought over who would hold him as a baby; Ed Turner took Jethro and Jenny during the period of illness that killed three of the other children; even though Ed Turner was quite young, he took good care of them; twin girl sisters, Lydia and Lucinda, had married and moved to Ohio; Jenny had rocked baby Matt's cradle too hard and rolled him out onto the floor; Benjamin had left for California in 1849 in search of gold.

3. Jenny now fears Shad will be killed, and she hesitates to plan a future with him.
4. Sam Gardiner, expecting a break-in or attack by Guy Wortman, hides in wait in his dark store each night. When nothing happens, he lets it be known he is going to St. Louis on business and will be gone a week. However, at the first train stop an accomplice secretly brings him back to his store, where he hides in his loft for three days. When Guy Wortman and his group pry open the store window and begin destroying things, Sam hits Guy Wortman's backside with a blast of buckshot. The neighbors have a good laugh, and Wortman is finally silenced.
5. While Halleck's soldiers slowly advance, digging entrenchments along the way, Beauregard's men secretly leave Corinth, leaving behind some dummy cannons and a few drummers. When Halleck arrives at the deserted city, he occupies it and claims it as "a victory as brilliant and important as any recorded in history."
6. Dave Burdow cuts a load of logs and sends them to the Creightons. Following his ride with Jethro on his return from Newton, several neighbors have shaken hands with him in appreciation of his efforts.
7. Answers will vary in depth, but should mention at least three of these generals and an acceptable summary of what they did: *McClellan*—Antietam—Restored confidence and courage to the troops; a northern victory which cost a great many lives; was later relieved of his command. *Pope*—Bull Run (2nd battle)—After early victories at New Madrid and the Confederate Fort at Island 10, the northern army under Pope's command was disorganized and demoralized and suffered defeat, resulting in many desertions. *Farragut*—New Orleans—Northern victory under seemingly impossible circumstances. *Grant*—Pittsburg Landing—Was criticized for not entrenching his soldiers; suffered defeat and was reduced to assistant commander; known as a heavy drinker. *Rosecrans*—Corinth (2nd battle) and Stones River—Defeated the south against Van Dorn and led a northern victory against General Bragg.
8. Soldiers become discouraged and are losing faith in their leaders and in the cause of unity. Many fear the once-mighty nation will remain as two weak ones.
9. Hunt juxtaposes the shooting of Guy Wortman and his subsequent humiliation and General Halleck traveling too slowly to capture the southern troops in the quickly evacuated Corinth. When he does take the empty town, Halleck boasts of his brilliant and important victory. This comparison may be pointing out that men can be ridiculous and braggarts no matter what their position or importance.
10. a. The cabin is compared to an old man.
b. Their idea of him (their opinion) is compared to something bitter to swallow.
Dig Deeper:
11. Answers will vary. Jethro makes no comment, feeling that it would be disrespectful to contradict an adult. He is self-controlled, patient, and respectful of his elders. He recognizes the sacrifice the men are making in order to help his family.
12. Jethro's attitude reflects 1 Corinthians 13 in that he is patient and kind and is not rude to adults. As a child, he might have let his anger get the best of him in this situation, but he has chosen to respond in a proper adult manner.
13. Shad considers McClellan a brave and a devoted leader. However, although McClellan restores confidence and courage to his soldiers, Shad senses McClellan is afraid of sending soldiers to their death or of losing their good opinion. Shad also feels he lacks the singleness of purpose necessary to win the war. He considers Burnside to be stubbornly self-righteous because he sent thousands to their death in a matter of minutes in a cruel and futile battle.
14. Scripture commands us to be obedient to those in authority over us, to not slander, to show humility, and to be ready to do whatever is good. Shad has been obedient to his generals. He has fought courageously. His comments, while critical, are not stated disrespectfully nor slanderously.

Chapters 9 & 10

Vocabulary:
1. disdain, scorn, derision; 2. adventurer, daredevil, criminal, bully; 3. compel, enforce, conscript; 4. raid, attack, sudden assault; 5. bold, impertinent, insolent, snotty (slang); 6. hopefulness, enthusiasm, anticipation; 7. mockery, jokes, disrespect; 8. thought, wondering, contemplation
a. ridicule; b. draft; c. contempt; d. impudent; e. optimistic
Questions:
1. A deserter is a soldier who has left his unit without permission and is now a fugitive from the law. Point Prospect campground becomes a hideout for between 100 and 500 deserters who raid nearby fields and farms for food. These are desperate men, determined to protect their identities, who might even resort to murder if someone recognizes one of

them. Several of them seem to have murdered a man who bragged about paying someone else to take his place in the military. It is a place of fear for the community, and even the Federal registrars do not go there.
2. Nancy closes her house and moves in with the Creightons, and Jenny is no longer permitted to drive to Hidalgo alone. Nobody goes out after dark; a sense of fear and foreboding hangs over the family and the community.
3. A man could purchase a substitute for $300 if he had dependent motherless children to care for, if there were serious illness in the home which required his presence, or other extenuating circumstances. However, some men twisted this to their own advantage even when they did not qualify.
4. They are to contact the Federal registrars in Chicago to report his whereabouts. Failure to do so could bring serious trouble on the family.
5. Shad is seriously wounded and his wounds become gangrenous, threatening his life. He is brought from Gettysburg to a Washington hospital, where his aunt is a volunteer nurse, and she discovers him there. She cares for him and writes to Matt Creighton asking for Jenny to come, offering to pay Jenny's expenses as well as housing her while she remains.
6. Ross Milton convinces Matt that Jenny's presence with Shad might be the 1-in-100 chance for his recovery—he promises to take her there and provide for her safety. Matt feels he can't let Jenny suffer any more if there is even a small hope of her reaching Shad while he is still alive or of her helping him to survive.
7. Jethro visits the schoolhouse and spends time in Shad's room. He finds filth and disorder left by the substitute teacher. This angers him, and he determines to clean the place for Shad's eventual return.
8. Jenny's presence offers hope, cheer, and comfort. She helps care for them as the nurses instruct her; she makes soup and bread and distributes these to the wounded.
Thinking About the Story:
9. Answers may vary. Eb is saying that while in battle he has a chance of surviving the battle, but that in deserting he has given himself a death sentence. Eb and the other deserters are desperate because the penalty for desertion is death. If any of them are caught by the authorities, they will be hung or shot.
10. Answers will vary. Some possibilities follow: Turn Eb In: The law requires it; the family could get in trouble if he didn't; loyalty to men who'd died or continued fighting; what if everyone quit. Let Eb Go Free: Eb is family, and he can't turn his back on family; he can't imagine the pressures Eb was under; he feels unfit to judge Eb.
11. Answers may vary—in fact, the student may be able to make a strong case for all three types of irony. A case may be made that the statement is dramatic irony because the reader and Jethro can see that the reality is different from what the man believes. However, it could also be labeled general irony because 11-year-old boys *should* be free of the worries of war, just as the man said, but they aren't. It demonstrates verbal irony when Jethro makes fun of the idea of being a carefree child after quoting the man. Not only did Jethro worry about the war, whether his brothers were safe, and whether those at home would be protected, but he also had taken on the full responsibility of providing a living for the family members still at home. Now he has the added burden of caring secretly for Eb and trying to decide the best course of action.
Dig Deeper:
12. Answers will vary, accept reasonably supported answers. Even though Jethro's motives were good—protecting his father from stress and his family from worry—he was really too young to take all the responsibility upon himself. He should have gone to them for wise counsel.
13. These verses teach us that many advisors help our plans succeed, a friend loves at all times and a brother helps in adversity, we should make plans with advice and guidance, and make good plans so you can finish what you begin. Jethro should have sought help, advice, and support from his friends and family. His parents could have provided wisdom beyond Jethro's years. Ironically, some of these verses could also lead Jethro *to* the decision he made: by taking on the burden himself, he would be helping his brother in adversity, and by writing to Lincoln he was seeking good counsel. Sometimes wise words can be applied in multiple ways.
14. Mercy, for Eb, means everything. He will have his life back and no longer be an outcast and wanted man. This is a verse that explains that judgment without mercy will be the fate of those who show no mercy. Mercy triumphs over judgment. Just as God is merciful to us when we don't deserve it, so we are to be merciful to others even when they don't deserve it. We must forgive when they don't deserve to be forgiven. Lincoln decided to offer complete forgiveness to all deserters even though they didn't deserve it and others would question his decision.
15. Answers will vary; accept reasonable responses. Matthew had been against Jenny marrying Shad until she went to Washington to be with him. It may be that her father saw in her letters that she had grown and was ready for marriage.

Both Jenny and Jethro seem far more mature than most people their ages—this is probably because of the war and the hardships they have been through. Most 11-year-old boys do not have to take care of their families; doing so makes a person mature very quickly. Going through the worries of war and having friends and relatives wounded and die make young people grow up faster than is usual.

Connections With History:

4. Hooker vs. Lee, battle at Chancellorsville, VA, Confederate victory. Rosecrans vs. Bragg, battle at Chickamauga/Chattanooga, TN, Union retreat to Chattanooga. Grant vs. Pemberton, battle at Vicksburg, Union victory. Meade vs. Lee, battle at Gettysburg, PA, Union victory.

Chapters 11 & 12

Vocabulary:

1. irreparable; 2. complicity; 3. obscurity; 4. annals; 5. pandemonium; 6. tranquil; 7. vindictiveness; 8. jubilation; 9. paeans; 10. amnesty. Accept reasonable usage of these words in sentences.

Questions:

1. Jethro learns that Chickamauga was a terrible defeat for the Union armies. Although George Thomas ("the Rock of Chickamauga") held firmly against Bragg, forcing him to give up, Rosecrans, McCook, and Crittenden had lost control of their men in the mountains.
2. Some were critical of the speech, calling it "silly, flat, dish-watery utterances." Others said it would "live among the annals of men." Ellen thought it sounded like Scripture passages.
3. Lincoln, a Republican, favored clemency toward the South and readmission of states to the Union. McClellan, a Democrat, said the North was not to offer peace except by reestablishment of the Union. Others in the Democrat party held the position of "no mercy to the South."
4. The neighbor's reactions were mixed, but the student may mention: Some felt the South deserved no mercy; some reveled in the destruction. It would bring scars to the nation; it was justified because of the South's mistreatment of prisoners at Andersonville; they crossed over the line of decency. Ed Turner worried that his son was praised for the acts of death and destruction, fearing it would damage his character development.

Thinking About the Story:

5. A Confederate state could return to the Union whenever 10% of its voters reestablished a loyal Union government; any individual Confederate who would swear to protect the Constitution and the Union and to abide by the government's stand against slavery would receive pardon and full rights of citizenship.
6. Jethro remembers Lincoln's former statement of his desire to "err on the side of mercy," and Jethro seems to approve.
7. Milton fears that, for the next 50 years, freed slaves will still be looking for their promised freedom and the ability to make a living for themselves; and the many who have known only slavery, who are uneducated and unskilled, will be exploited.
8. Both men see the problem of northern abolitionists who, at the same time they wanted to free the slaves, would not extend a hand to help freed slaves get back on their feet or begin to build a new life. They both understand the prejudice that exists in the hearts of men, and they know that the North would be reluctant to admit freed slaves into its society.
9. Bill is taken as a prisoner of war to John's camp. John secures permission from his captain to speak to Bill, and the two speak as brothers once again, talking about family and life at home. Bill wants Ma to know he had not been at Pittsburg Landing where Tom was killed. Answers will vary, but the family might have felt some renewed pain at the reminder of Bill's fighting for the Southern cause, as well as relief knowing he could not have been responsible directly for his brother's death. They surely are relieved to hear that Bill is alive, as well as John. John hopes Bill's message will bring a measure of comfort.
10 a. his face was <u>full of light</u>, M; b. country <u>will not admit that its sons</u>, P; c. expect peace to be <u>a perfect pearl</u>, M; d. the fifth April had become, like <u>her four older sisters</u>, P; e. the <u>soft golden blanket</u> of sunlight, M
11a. <u>the plainest and the most beautiful</u>, <u>the humblest and the most magnificent</u>; b. <u>joy for the living, grief for the dead</u>
12. Answers may vary, but may mention the soldiers burning Columbia and laughing, looting, mirrors and pianos smashed, heirlooms destroyed. Ed Turner fears that his son will become hardened, that human life will become cheap, and that he will learn to laugh at distress, and to smash the helpless without pity.
13. The land is lying in physical and spiritual destruction. There is also widespread hatred and thirst for revenge to worry about. He worries more about the spiritual damage than the physical damage.

14. Ross Milton and Jethro put their hope for real peace in Abraham Lincoln. Jethro and the people are devastated and grieving over Lincoln's death.
15. Ross Milton fears for all the men and women who will be free but with nowhere to go, no experience, and no education. He recognizes that the Amendment will change their legal status but not the bigotry people feel toward them, and he fears many will try to exploit them.
Dig Deeper:
16. Answers may vary. Sherman's army destroyed everything in its path on its march through Georgia. They burned every building they could, stole or destroyed all livestock, stole or destroyed anything of value they could find. They destroyed roads, railways, and telegraph lines, leaving little upon which the South could start rebuilding after the war. The army preyed upon anything and anyone its path—rich and poor, young and old, strong and helpless. We now call this a "scorched earth" policy.
17. Answers may vary. The literary term is "juxtaposition"—Hunt first shows us the well-fed, comfortable northern farmers and city dwellers and gives us some of their complaints and justifications for Sherman's actions before she reveals the full horror of their destruction. By telling us how comfortable the people are in the Midwest and juxtaposing this with the total destruction of Sherman's march, she in some ways invalidates their complaints and bitterness. These people still have things pretty good compared to those actually in the war and especially compared to those who lost everything to Sherman's army. The technique is very effective here.
18. Psalms teaches us that God is gracious, abounding in love, He does not hold onto His anger or treat us as we deserve. Luke teaches us to love our enemies, to be giving, to be kind even to enemies, without expecting anything back. Romans tells us to live at peace with everyone. Colossians tells us to be compassionate and kind, to completely forgive all grievances just as God forgives us. We are called to be peaceful. 1 Peter teaches us to live in peace with one another, be kind, loving, do *not* be insulted, but bless others. Seek peace and pursue it.

Overview
1. The main conflict in *Across Five Aprils* is the American Civil War and the fighting that occurs both on the battlefront and at home in their own town.
2. Jethro's brothers choose different sides to join in the war, causing stress and grief at home and with neighbors. Jethro's father has a heart attack making him unable to work the farm, thereby forcing Jethro to shoulder the load of all the farmwork and care of the family. Shad is badly injured and Tom is killed.
3. The climax occurs as the war ends, then Lincoln is assassinated.
4. We find out what has happened to each brother, and Shadrach returns home. John will be returning in few weeks, and Jethro will get to go to school.
5. The conflict is in the form of man vs. man, though there are some instances of man vs. himself, such as when Bill struggles about joining the southern army and Jethro struggles about what to do concerning Eb.
6. Irene Hunt uses the month of April to evoke a sense of growth, new life, and renewal—a continuation of life despite the events around them. Jethro must grow and renew, just like the seasons do, as he matures despite, but also as a result of, the events around him. Answers may vary.
7. Answers may vary. The passages in Psalms specifically tell us to not trust in princes and military might; they will fail us, but God will not. Both the passages in Daniel and Romans tell us that though earthly rulers may have authority over our bodies, nothing can separate us from God's love and authority and so we must obey him. Earthly rulers and authorities may promise many things, and they may try hard to provide them, but men will always disappoint us. Even Abraham Lincoln, as sincere as he was and as hard as he tried, was unable to fulfill all that he wished simply because he was a mortal man and someone killed him. Even if he had lived, however, he may not have been able to do all that people hoped simply because he did not have the power to make things happen the way he wished. If he had, he would have stopped the war. Note particularly Romans 8:28, in which Paul says, "in all things God works for the good of those who love him." Not all things are good, but in all things God works for the good—whatever happens is working together with other things to be for our best. No one else can promise that much.